Drunken Soul

Overcoming Addictions & Discovering the Power of Real Breakthrough

Lavonia L. Mack-Crawford

Extreme Overflow Publishing
Dacula, GA
USA

Extreme Overflow Publishing
Dacula, GA
USA

Extreme Overflow Publishing
A Brand of Extreme Overflow Enterprises, Inc
P.O. Box 1811
Dacula, GA 30019

www.extremeoverflow.com
Send feedback to info@extreme-overflow-enterprises.com

Printed in the United States of America

Library of Congress Catalogin-Publication
Data is available for this title. ISBN: 978-1-7340638-4-4

Drunken Soul

Lavonia L Mack-Crawford

Table of Contents

* * *

Introduction

drunken soul is one that is weak, defenseless, and incapable of protecting itself due to a virus like invasion that entered the soulish area of a person. A drunken soul is one that is governed not by alcohol, per se, but by strongholds, evil spirits, and demonic influences. Those who suffer from a drunken soul must take heed to the Bible when it tells us to guard our heart with all diligence, because out of the heart flows the issues of life.

Think about the behavior of a person when they're intoxicated. They are usually loud and their speech is slurred. These behaviors come from the high level of alcohol present in the person's bloodstream. The symptoms of an intoxicated person and a person with a drunken soul are similar. When a person has a drunken soul, it is as if they are drunk in the natural; they're unable to protect themselves, just like an intoxicated person. The two are the same, just the poison is different. One is a natural poison, and the other is a spiritual poison. Both produce the same outcome; needing deliverance and recovery.

I compare a drunken soul with a person drunken with alcohol because it illustrates the parallel nature of the spirit and natural nature. When abused overtime, alcohol inside of the human body can become toxic and destroy your system. Just as strongholds, evil spirits, and demonic influences in the body can cause destruction, there are so many people in the world today that have lost their souls to drunkenness. They are controlled by something they can't touch, taste, see, smell, nor feel. How can you fight something you cannot lay your hands on? Here's a secret. Ok, it's not a secret! There is an adversary out to destroy mankind. It does not care about anything except its agenda! It's out to destroy you because of your creator. It wants to destroy everything made by the creator!

The spirit of destruction hates everything with the

potential to grow! It's on the warpath to destroy you any way it can. One way is drugs. So many people indulge in illegal and prescription drugs. I was inspired to write this book by the inspiration of the Holy Spirit, in addition to a question asked of me. This question isn't easy to reply to when the person asking is unaware of God's knowledge, wisdom, and his ways. The question presented to me as a believer, "Why does God permit suffering?"

Jesus has the answers to every question and for every question, there is an answer. I pray by the time you finish reading this book you would have an understanding to the question of "why." The most powerful weapon I use to help individuals, especially children I encounter, is prayer! The power of prayer works! In this instance, I pray and pray more for the effective prayer of the righteous that avails much. Every day when facing challenges due to the suffering that individuals and children must endure requires believers to be vigilant in how we respond. The answer the Holy Spirit gave was to say that we must rise up and be a part of the solution. According to Romans 8:19, for those amongst us are waiting for the children of God to rise up with power and solutions. The whole world is waiting for the true sons of God to come forth with the wisdom of God. If you are not a part of the solution, you are a part of the problem. God's wisdom helps us to find peace when this question of suffering in the world is asked.

One avenue of suffering today is the destructive power of drugs. Drug usage is on the incline and destroying the lives of mothers, fathers, daughters, and sons. Many souls are lost in hell because of drug abuse. Although people know the dangers of drug abuse, they continue to consciously use. This is a demonstration of a spirit of rebelliousness and with rebelliousness comes the spirit of addiction. When you are rebelling, you might hear within your mind: "It is okay. Nothing is going to happen. You're not going to get addicted, try it. Go ahead, just try it. Everyone else is doing it." Or maybe you've convinced yourself that you'll only try it once. Or that you're strong and only weak people become addicted to drugs. "It will make you feel good," you might hear. The devil is a deceiver. When what you fail to hear is the truth, you can become hooked on your very first try. Or continue to use until you are unable to stop of your own free will.

Of course, your adversary isn't going to tell you the

truth. He wants you to continue to use drugs until you're well addicted, and you are unable to break loose. But all the while, you are thinking, I can stop any time I want to. The truth is you can't! There's a stronghold in your life and you must break it. How? With spiritual weapons!

A stronghold is the mental beliefs built up within the mind. It is how you think. A simply illustration of a stronghold is like a fortress with a strong reinforced wall to keep everything inside on lock down, therefore nothing in or nothing out. Everything on the inside is protected. It's a fortress built up in your mind to keep you in a certain place within your belief system or/ thought life.

Strongholds are of a spiritual nature; therefore, it will take spiritual weapons to tear it down. How? Through the WORD of GOD, you must renew your mind Romans 12:1-2. You must learn to replace wrong stinky beliefs with righteous thinking.

For the weapons of our spiritual warfare are not carnal (not physical weapons), but mighty through God to the pulling down (destroying) of strong holds. (2 Corinthians 10: 4).Put on the spiritual armor of protection to fight against your adversary. In this season, you must be spiritually ready and armed. (Ephesians 6: 10-18).

Take back what the adversary has stolen from you; your Liberty! In Jesus' name. Amen!

Suffering

* * *

When a person's soul is drunk, it is in pain. The only way of healing the soul is by healing the spirit. During my monthly get together with my co-workers, two of them asked me, "Why does God allow little children to suffer?" First, God isn't to blame for the suffering. God tells us, He is love and He came to give life, not take it. Therefore, where does the suffering come from? We must go back to the beginning of time for the answer. God gave man free will to choose to follow good (life) or evil (death). When man chose to follow evil, he paid the cost for his decision; for the wages of sin is death. As a result of sin, something will die in your life. Adam, before he sinned, was spiritually like God. He was able to function like God because Adam and God were spiritually connected. When Adam disobeyed

God, it did not only affect Adam, it also affected his entire family and offspring. Adam's sins brought sin upon his children, his children's children, and upon all generations to come, for we are descendants of Adam.

When sin arrived, it brought with it a nature that's unrighteous, unholy, and ungodly. A fallen nature entered into the heart and soul of mankind. After the fall of Adam, the soul of man changed, and the spirit of man was disconnected from the Father. Man was no longer able to be led or live by his spirit; he is now led and living by his soul and body. Thank God for Jesus, because he came to restore man to the position man held with the Father before sin arrived. Man's spirit is what lives forever. The soul of a man may perish, but the spirit of a man lives on. Healing the spirit connects it back to the Father through the gift of salvation. Without salvation, man is lost.

Satan wants the soul of a man, because he knows if he gets the soul, he has the person in bondage. Satan holds you in an eternal death with him. Satan and man's disobedience cause the world suffering. The war that continues to go on around the world year after year is because of man. It is because of man's desires, man's greed, and man's own strong selfish will due to man not listening. Instead, man chooses the wrong thing, and through that wrong decision there are negative consequences and when the outcome is negative it causes great devastation to families, nations, and communities.

Soul Cleaning

* * *

Society says to God that we do not want you in our business and have also removed God from our public sector. For example, there is no prayer in schools. We can't have it both ways. It's a shame when tragedy hits our nation we remember God. In the same breath, some blame God for the tragedy taking place. You can't have it both ways. It's either he's in or out. I pray he's in and you let him clean your soul.

Drunken souls will have to be dipped and washed in the blood of Jesus. When you dip something and take it out, it becomes encased. The same happens when the soul is being cleansed, it becomes encased by the Blood of Jesus. That gray and dim spirit can't live where the Spirit of God – the blood, is applied! The way this world is today, people do not take the time to get "dipped," or rehearse their decisions, so they can determine the safest decision. People try and come up with the right decisions in a split second. Important decisions should be pondered over, and not just for a couple of minutes. It takes time, hours, days, weeks, and even months. Especially, if it could cause harm to your child, and family.

Your decisions not only affect you, but everyone around you. One decision can change your life forever. In addition to taking time to meditate on the decisions you have made in life, you can also pray! If you believe in Jesus, go into prayer! It will cleanse your soul. Ask Him what is the best decision to make, because He knows all, including the safest path to take to free your soul from bondage! Jesus will either tell you what to decide, or He'll assist you through your decision process. Also, think your decisions through. If I choose this, think about what will happen. Is this the expected outcome of what I want it to be?

You will be surprised how many people do not take the time out to think about the consequences of their decisions, and what those decisions might cost. The consequences are either going to be good and helpful to your family, or bad and harmful to your family. You can't blame God; blame the person and the roots of the problem. All it takes is one person. One person can make a difference. Just one can! Jesus died all by Himself; my Lord was alone. He stood on the word of the Father and destroyed death! Even you can make a difference.

When Satan plants the question in our mind, "Why does God allow suffering?" Let's decide to stop the suffering together! Ask God how you can make a difference and be a part of the solution and not the problem.

Rescue My Soul

* * *

A drunken soul is a soul in turmoil. When someone possesses a drunken soul, they need to seek Jehovah-Rophe, otherwise known as the God of healing. These spirits are strong and not easily moved. When people have personal issues in their life, they need spiritual deliverance. You must tap into the word and His anointing. God said in His word, "This kind can only come forth by prayer and fasting." (Mark 9:23). For every issue or area in your life, the word of God is the answer. Maybe you've been through rehab several times but still can't seem to break your addiction. Even though your mind and heart are willing, the flesh might be weak. Unless you fill your spirit with the strength of God's word, you will not be able to break chains, unlock, or sober up your drunken soul.

Rehab feeds your soul, not your spirit. They may replace illegal street drugs with legally addicting medication. The mental hospitals are full of adults and children. They provide them with therapy and food for the soul and body. They provide them with medication which many are harmful to the body.

There is one substance that is extremely harmful to the body, if abused. Alcohol! Alcohol wasn't meant to be addictive and abused. Jesus' first miracle was turning water into wine; because of Satan and sin, people lose their souls to it. God never intended for the world to exist in a drunken state, bound and broken.

Satan won't dare go against himself and reveal to the world that he is the one causing suffering. Satan wants you to blame God for all that goes wrong in the world. Satan wants you to question God through doubting with questions like, "How could God allow this to happen?" Do not allow Satan to fill your mind with all sorts of questions about suffering, addictions, and children suffering. Instead of focusing your attention on who is to blame, focus on the solution. If you are willing, Jesus will use you as the solution; you, and you are the solution. That's how the village grows.

How can you be set free? I encourage you to seek spiritual guidance. Pray that the Holy Spirit will direct your steps into the right directions. Pray He will direct you to an anointed church with a great deliverance ministry. Along with counseling to address deep wounds (hurts) of wounded memories, some addictions are due to self-medicating wounded emotions. To cover and submerge the emotions from feeling the unwanted, undesired pain. There is trauma living within the soul that needs to be set free. You need healing! You must understand, not every church is called by God; therefore, you want to be led to the right house of God. (Isaiah 56: 7, Matthew 21: 13)

Break the Binds

* * *

*T*o come out of a drunken soul stooper, you need to be surrounded by prayer warriors who has taken up the armor of God, and filled with the Holy Spirit, and speak in tongues. (Romans 8:26) We all need people to intercede for us, especially when we are in a battle. You must begin to rebuke that stronghold of addiction in your life and feed your spirit with God's word on healing and strength. It's going to take spiritual warfare to destroy that stronghold.

When you repent and cry out for help, that demon isn't going to want to release his grip from your life. He will want to hold on tighter. But fill your belly (your inner man) with God's word, and let that be your strength. Fill up on it! Pray and allow God to fill you with His spirit and operate your source of strength, which is the Holy

Spirit. Pray in the spirit. Your mind is subject to your spirit through praying in the spirit. When you pray in the spirit your mind is unaware of what you are speaking. Therefore, the devil is unable to launch an attack against you. The gift of speaking in an unknown tongue cuts through the enemies' barriers (Acts 2: 8 and Mark 16: 15). Speak in your beautiful heavenly language and your life will never be the same!

From this day forward, confess your deliverance and believe that you are healed. Know that God has put something amazing inside of you that is revealed through the studying of His word. His word is life. The more you study it, the more it is going to take root in your spirit.

As God is strengthening your spirit, your soul releases the addictive spirit holding you in bondage. To free your soul, you need to heal your soul. To do that, you need God's help and anointing. God wants you to be free from the enemy's traps. It is not necessary for you to feel empty and try to fill voids in your life with drugs, sex, food, alcohol, shopping, or anything that is not of God.

Jesus is the best addiction you or I could ever consider

having. The devil sowed you lies, and your lifestyle reveals the lies that the devil sowed to you. Are you living a fulfilling life free from the addition of drugs? Do not lie to yourself any longer. Stop saying to yourself, "I can quit anytime I get ready to!" If that were true, then the real question is, why haven't you? I'll tell you the answer. Because you bought into the lies the enemy sold to you!

Maybe you said you were going to quit 5, 10, 15, or even 25 years ago, but you are still using. If that's you, you're also in denial! You have lost your family, your home, job, everything. You are holding onto the lies Satan planted in your mind, which has turned into a stronghold in your life. Let go of the lies; I come against every lie in Jesus' name! Let them go and allow God to uproot the spirit of addiction out of your weak and frail body. Let Him create in you divine health, supernatural strength, and courage. You do not need a crush. Allow God to be your crush. Isaiah 41: 10 tells us that He will be there for you and will strengthen you. God will not hurt you or lie to you. You can trust Him!

Go through God's rehab and walk out a new person. Show that unclean addictive spirit that the only thing you are ever going to be addicted to is the blood of Jesus. Stand your ground with the enemy and say no more, no more lies! You must take back your life! Your soul doesn't belong to Satan.It doesn't belong in hell. (Ezekiel 18: 4) Your spirit knows. It reveals the truth to you and what course of action you should take. It reveals it to your mind, and soul when it's impacted by the word of God and changes your life. If you do not align your body, mind, and soul up with the word of God, it is going to fail you. It's going to keep you bound in addiction.

The heart is willing but the flesh is weak (Matthew 26:41). Your flesh gives way all the time. You cannot trust in the flesh because that is Satan's dwelling place. You must keep your flesh under wraps and in line with the Word of God. That's the only way you're going to keep your flesh from remaining a drunken soul. You must ask the Holy Spirit to create in you a clean heart. You must line up your life with God's word by renewing your mind Romans 12: 2, which will transform your life and modify your behaviors. Do you want to live in heaven on earth? You can, it is possible! Jesus came so we might have life more abundantly (John 10: 10). Make up in your heart and mind; then decide whether you're going to go through nine months, or even 12 months of detox! Ask the Lord to strengthen you, because this will be the last time you ever deal with this demon of addiction again!

Then, the hell you've lived here on earth will change to heaven on earth! You must see yourself with a new life, set free of addiction, loneliness, emptiness, rejection, abandonment, and depression. You must see yourself already free! See yourself walking out God's will for your life! See yourself walking in victory! See yourself a winner! See yourself as an overcomer! See yourself whole and complete! (Colossians 2: 10) See yourself as Christ sees you! Just like Him!

Satan sowed seeds of destruction in your life but God sows seeds of joy, love, fulfillment, purpose, peace, temperance, acceptance, blessings, and so much more.

Resist the devil with the word of God. Know that you are not alone and you do not have to go through your struggles alone. Make God and His word the power you use to take out the mountains in your life.

Open the Bible and begin to read God's word and pray it back to Him (1 John 5: 14-15)! Allow God's word to minister to you, to your heart, and your mind. When both heart and mind are in line with God's word, you are on your way to total victory over your flesh and over yoursoul.

Remember, what God says comes to past when it becomes real to your spirit. Let the word be ingrafted within you, "out of the heart flows the issues of life." (Proverbs 4: 23) "Fear not for I'm with you," says the Lord (Isaiah 41: 10)! That's your foundation to stand on against the enemy's temptations. Pray when the temptation arises. When that craving is raging war on the inside of you to be feed, instead of feeding your fleshly desire, feed your spirit man the word!

God must clean out everything that Satan tricked you into letting inside of your drunken soul. Your system must be flushed out. For every pain that you feel, know that God is breaking you loose from the stronghold the enemy held you in bondage to. God feels every pain with you because He is touched by our infirmities. God felt that pain when He sent His only begotten son to die on the cross for you. (John 3: 16).

Beloved, He is saying to you, "Know that every pain you feel while going through detox is the angels breaking away that unclean spirit of addiction." Do not let the enemy give you pain. Actually, you pain the enemy when you resist his addictive spirit. Do not let your flesh break you! You break it! Let your spirit continue to resist what you know is wrong! The Holy Spirit wants you to know and remember the pain, because the memory of the pain reminds us that we don't ever want to go through this hell again. Remember what you went through to get free? Don't you dare forget the pain in that process! You can forget everything else, but not the pain, nor the misery of getting clean. Satan won't dare remind you of the pain. He only reminds you of the so-called fun you had. Yes, so-called fun!

That so-called fun in hindsight more than likely ruined your life and caused you pain. If you give in to temptation again after being delivered from that unclean addictive spirit, it's going to return stronger, and with seven more demons (Matthew 12: 45). Remember the hell you went through the first time to get free? Well, it is going to be seven times harder the second time around to get free, because you now have seven more demons tormenting you. You may even find yourself engaging in greater immoral activities than before. You might find yourself doing things you would've never done before, but now you are! Why? The demons are stronger, and the first demon is reinforced by even stronger evil spirits.

Do not fall for Satan's tricks or his temptations; run, run! Do not walk away. Satan will surely walk with you. Run! He cannot catch you because you have God's shoes of speed upon your feet (Ephesians 6: 12). It's hard to keep up with a moving target. Do not be a target for Satan anymore. Do not go where you used to hang out. Do not socialize with the people you used to hang out with. If they are not free from addiction, they will only pull you back into the lifestyle. Ask God to deliver you from your old surroundings. Remember you may be in this world, but you're not of this world (I John 4: 4). Break all familiar spirits off your life.

Closing: Say Goodbye to the Old Self

● ● ●

I pray that God direct you to the right facility for rehabilitation and counseling. I pray He directs you to a place where there are anointed and God-fearing people available to assist you in your transformation towards deliverance and recovery. Total recovery is possible! Mark 10: 23 says, "With God all things are possible!" You want to be connected to a ministry that will teach you about the power of the Holy Spirit. They will also teach you the weapons to use against the enemy in your moments of weakness. If you have made up in your mind to get clean, pray this prayer by faith right now for strength and guidance.

Pray The Prayer Of Salvation

* * *

*F*ather, I accept the gift of salvation that you have given to me through your son Jesus. I believe Jesus is the Messiah. Lord I am asking you to forgive me for all my sins (knowingly and unknowingly) and to come and live inside of my heart. I make this confession by faith because of Romans 10: 8-10. Thank you, Father!

Father, in the mighty name of Jesus, I come to you now and ask you for your strength and guidance; that you may lead me to the place of deliverance and recovery.

Father, you know all about me, and you know what it will take for me to get clean. I trust in you Lord, and your word for my recovery; and as I pray this prayer, you make a way for me now. Recovery belongs to me now!

You are cutting asunder the cords of the enemy in my life. I know, Father, that I'm in line with your word, and

I have confidence that you will answer my prayers.

I have confidence that you are with me as I go through this journey, and every other journey that I must face. I know now that I'm never alone because your presence is with me.

Spirit of addiction, I cancel and nullify your assignment against my life; I bind the strongman of addiction and bondage over my life. I bind and rebuke you from interfering with my life. Satan, I'm taking back the powers I gave to you concerning my life. I'm now handing over the power of my life to Jesus Christ, who is Lord! I am Loosed!

I'm now a brand-new person in Jesus' name. Amen!

Authors Information

* * *

avonia was raised on the westside of Chicago with her mother and two siblings in addition to having 3 other siblings outside of the home. She attended Carl Schurz High School and Central Memorial Baptist Church where she accepted Christ at an early age. As a child, Lavonia began to experience the gifts of a Seer. But as she grew in age she would turn away from the church and experience the curves, the highs, the lows, the bumps, the failures, and the miseries of life.

Throughout all of the unhealthy choices that she would make, she never stopped believing in the one who created her, Jehovah God Almighty. At the age of 27, Lavonia had a life-altering encounter with the Holy Spirit. Frustrated with the mess and negative consequences of unhealthy decisions, Lavonia turned to the one she knew who could help and was drawn back to her first love, the Lord Jesus Christ!

Through prayer and studying the word of God Lavonia began to search out the will of God for her life. This took her down a journey of learning, healing, and deliverance. To her surprise, she learned that deliverance would be the very ministry that God would place upon her life to help others, the Ministry of Deliverance, the anointing to set the captives free and heal the brokenhearted (Luke 4:18). With the wisdom, knowledge, and understanding of God's word, today, Lavonia has committed her life to the service of God and those who are in need of spiritual guidance. She contributes much of her changed life to her mother's faithful and committed prayers and is thankful. Lavonia was once lost, but now she's found. The prodigal daughter has returned! Lavonia will continue to, "be strong in the Lord and in the power of

His might" (Ephesians 6:10). She will make it her life's work to honor God and break every demonic stronghold, in the Mighty Name of Jesus, AMEN!

God will give you the ability to heal from the inside out and empower you to trust in His love to change your life forever.

For booking or for more information contact:
Lavoniaspeaks@gmail.com

www.ingramcontent.com/pod-product-compliance
Lightning Source LLC
Chambersburg PA
CBHW071652040426
42452CB00009B/1840